A
Bowater
Album

By David Hammersley

Noodle Books

A Bowater's Album

Title Page and Above: *My first sight of Bowater's railway. Kerr Stuart 0-4-2ST 'Melior' raises steam. Years of hard industrial use have given the corrugated iron shed building at Sittingbourne a ramshackle air. Sited on the lower, wharf level it was surrounded by paper store sheds, pulp stacks and china clay heaps. The far shed road is elevated within the building to ease maintenance without a pit. Tracks in front of the building led to the wharfside and storage areas. 6/7/67*

Right: *At the far end of the line the wide variety of motive power owned by Bowater's is demonstrated. The massive Bagnall 0-6-2T 'Conqueror' shunts carriages for the afternoon passenger train at Ridham Dock, terminus of the 2ft 6in gauge Bowater's Light Railway. The train will be returned to Sittingbourne by one of the slightly smaller Bagnall 0-6-2Ts while 'Conqueror' continues shunting the dockside and pulp stacks. 10/7/67*

© David Hammersley and Kevin Robertson (Noodle Books) 2009

ISBN 978 1 906419 26 4

First published in 2009 by Kevin Robertson
Under the NOODLE BOOKS imprint
PO Box 279
Corhampton
SOUTHAMPTON
SO32 3ZX

www.kevinrobertsonbooks.co.uk

Designed by David Hammersley, Tidemark Designs

Printed in England by
Information Press Ltd.
Eynsham

A Bowater's Album - Introduction

As a railway enthusiast I have always been drawn to the unusual and quirky, the odd bye-way, the industrial back water. When, in 1967, the Locomotive Club of Great Britain announced a visit to a large narrow gauge system in my home county of Kent I jumped at the chance.

So it was that I arrived at Bowaters paper mill in Sittingbourne for the first time. I was introduced to a fleet of handsome locos bustling around a vast network of tracks. Some were a little scruffy, but all were obviously well maintained and cared for.

The weather was perfect and every loco seemed determined to pose in just the right place for the sun. This sowed the seed for a lasting affection for the line, leading to two model railways based on it and to a small part in the first few years of its preservation.

The black and white pictures in this album were taken by myself on that first visit and a few others up to the handover to what became the Sittingbourne and Kemsley Light Railway. To fill gaps in the story I have included a few later views which show stock or features unaltered from their Bowaters appearance. Some earlier views are taken from negatives or original prints given to me at various times. Despite considerable enquiry I have been unable the photographers, so my apologies for not being able to credit them.

As a young graphic artist, fresh out of college, and in my first job, I could not afford colour film. I am therefore grateful to the gentlemen who have loaned transparencies for the colour section. They are credited by each picture.

Industrial railways are shaped by the business they serve and did not have the manicured finish of their mainline counterpart but still served a vital function in the process. I have tried to show in this album, not just the locos, but much of the surroundings which show other aspects of the paper making process. Bowater's railway was not just the smart Bagnall

side tanks or the Kerr Stuart 'Brazil's which seemed to appear round every corner. A large part of its character was formed by the large steam pipes which snaked alongside the line, leaping from side to side of it in great gantries; by the gargantuan stacks of wood pulp bales towering over everything except the even bigger cranes; by the aerial ropeway swishing overhead with bundles of logs which were dropped in conical piles with a sound like a giants game of ten pin bowling and by the background presence of Milton Creek with banks stained white with china clay and fallout from the local cement works and a smell to remember.

This part of North Kent is flat, marshy and windswept. The wide, almost treeless skyline only served to emphasise the huge scale of the Bowater's operation. The steam powered part of this came to an end in 1969 when all internal transport went over to road haulage. Several of the locomotives and pulp wagons were sold into preservation. The core of the locomotive fleet was leased to the Locomotive Club of Great Britain together with all the passenger coaches, a large selection of wagons and the track between Sittingbourne and Kemsley. This became the Sittingbourne and Kemsley Light Railway.

The story of the preservation society I will leave for others to tell, except to wish them well. In 2008 a succession of takeovers left them at the mercy of developers who wanted to sell the land the railway runs over. As I write thinks look much more positive and hopefully by the time you are reading this they will be running unhindered again. It would be a disaster to our heritage to lose a railway running the original rolling stock on its original line.

So join me for a trip round an industrial railway system of a type which has all but totally disappeared in this country, and indeed the world.

David Hammersley   July 2009

A Bowater's Album
A Brief History

A paper mill was set up in Sittingbourne by Edward Lloyd in the 19th century. It was sited between the main line of the London, Chatham and Dover Railway and the head of Milton Creek. This opened out into the Swale and then to the Thames and Medway estuaries. With sidings on the railway and wharves on the creek it had excellent transport connections to bring in raw materials such as timber, wood pulp, china clay and coal from London Docks, and to take out the finished paper.

Lloyds prospered and started to expand. In 1906 the first section of internal railway was laid from Sittingbourne Mill to the wharf on Milton Creek. It was laid to 2' 6" gauge, not common in the United Kingdom but a standard Colonial and military gauge of the era. Kerr Stuart supplied two 0-4-2Ts, 'Premier' and 'Leader' for the new railway, the first of what became a large and fascinating fleet. 'Excelsior' followed in 1908.

In 1913 construction commenced on building Ridham Dock at the mouth of Milton Creek, facing out into the Swale. This allowed ships to unload direct onto Lloyds property instead of the costly transhipment into barges for the trip up the creek to Sittingbourne. A new narrow gauge line was constructed to join the dock with Sittingbourne Mill, including the now famous concrete viaduct. The original wharf line became a spur off what was now the main line.

The First World War intervened, with Ridham Dock becoming a salvage depot. A famous wartime resident was standard gauge, ex LSWR Adams Radial Tank number 488, which is now preserved at the Bluebell Railway. Pictured with 488 at the same time was a narrow gauge Kerr Stuart 'Skylark' class 0-4-2T, which later appeared on the Snailbeach District Railway. Neither of these locos were owned by Lloyds.

No. 488 was sold from Ridham Dock in 1919 and went to the East Kent Light Railway. This is probably when the dock was finished and returned to Lloyds, for in 1920 'Superior' was delivered by Kerr Stuart. A well proportioned 0-6-2T, she would have been needed for the new 3.5 mile main line from Ridham Dock to Sittingbourne Mill. A year later an ungainly battery loco nicknamed 'The Tank' arrived from English Electric. This was for shunting in the warehouses of the dock area.

Traffic must have been booming as 'Conqueror' was delivered in 1922 and took over the main line workings. At the same time construction would have been proceeding with the huge new paper mill beside the line at Kemsley. This opened in 1924 with the delivery of two new locos, 'Melior' another Kerr Stuart 0-4-2T and 'Unique' which lived up to its name. It was a 2-4-0 fireless loco for shunting round the new mill.

The next arrival was also a fireless, 'Victor', which was delivered in 1929. Much smaller than 'Unique', she was one of the first Bowater's locos to be scrapped. Three more years brought the first of the trio of Bagnall 0-6-2T which dominated the Main Line workings until after World War Two. 'Alpha' was built in 1932, 'Triumph' in 1934 and 'Superb' in 1940.

Kemsley Mill and Ridham Dock had been connected to the mainline from the start and shunted by hired locos. In 1936 'Jubilee' arrived from Bagnall to do the job.

The next purchases were, unusually, second hand. 'Rattler' is very little documented. She arrived in 1942, possibly to alleviate a wartime motive power crisis and by 1945 she was derelict on Sittingbourne Wharf. In 1943 a reserve standard gauge loco 'Pioneer' appeared, but does not seem to have been successful. In 1950 another, more successful second hand loco arrived. 'Chevallier' came from the nearby Chattenden and Upnor

Railway operated by the Navy. Fitting in perfectly with the resident narrow gauge stock she worked until the end of the railway and survives in preservation.

The last brand new locos came in Coronation Year, 1953. One was a small four wheeled diesel from Hudson/Hunslet. This worked at Ridham Dock, possibly supplementing the battery loco in the paper storage sheds, where there would have been a high fire risk. Second was 'Monarch', an unusual Kitson-Meyer 0-4-4-0T articulated loco which ran the main line until sold in the early 1960s.

For many years Bowater's had been hiring standard gauge shunters from British Railways to assist 'Jubilee'. In 1958 P class 0-6-0T No. 31178 was purchased, repainted in full SECR lined livery and named Pioneer II. She worked alternate weeks with 'Jubilee'.

Bowater's finally dabbled with diesel traction on the standard gauge in 1969 when they bought a second hand 204hp shunter D2259 from British Railways. This was soon damaged in a shunting accident and replaced with a second, similar locomotive D2228.

The railway age at Bowater's came to an end in October 1969 when the Sittingbourne to Kemsley section of the main line, several of the locos and a representative selection of the rolling stock were handed over to the Locomotive Club of Great Britain. This was all on lease or loan from Bowater's and subsequent owners of the mills.

The line became The Sittingbourne and Kemsley Light Railway and its history is for others to tell. All the locomotives which survived to the end have found other homes in preservation, either on the Sittingbourne and Kemsley or other railways.

Above: *At first glance a very unusual view to put in a railway album, but full of fascinating industrial detail. The scene is the lower yard at Sittingbourne. The engine shed is behind me, in front is the permanent way store for the railway. Point levers are neatly lined up, lengths of rail and sleepers fill the area, two re-railing plates lean against a cabinet and a small trolley waits, off the track, to move them around.*
Behind this is the ugly, brick and concrete building in which I spent many hours signwriting for the SKLR. Beyond, but out of sight was the wharf and Milton Creek.
On the other side of the creek, and the intended subject of the photo, is 'Alpha'. She stands at the beginning of the famous concrete viaduct with two coaches for the workmans service and a rake of wagons as well. Also visible are two of the large gantries which carried steam pipes between Kemsley and Sittingbourne mills.

A Bowater's Album - Sittingbourne

Above: *'Melior' prepares for her last few duties under Bowater's ownership. The paintwork has had a wipe down with and oily rag, but fortyfive years of hard toil are hard to cover up. 4/10/69*

Left: *Kerr Stuart 0-4-2T 'Melior' raises steam outside Sittingbourne Shed in the morning. Shown to good effect is the large balloon type chimney that all the narrow gauge locos carried at various times for spark arresting. A lot of welding has been done on the smokebox door to keep her in service. 6/7/67*

A Bowater's Album - The Route

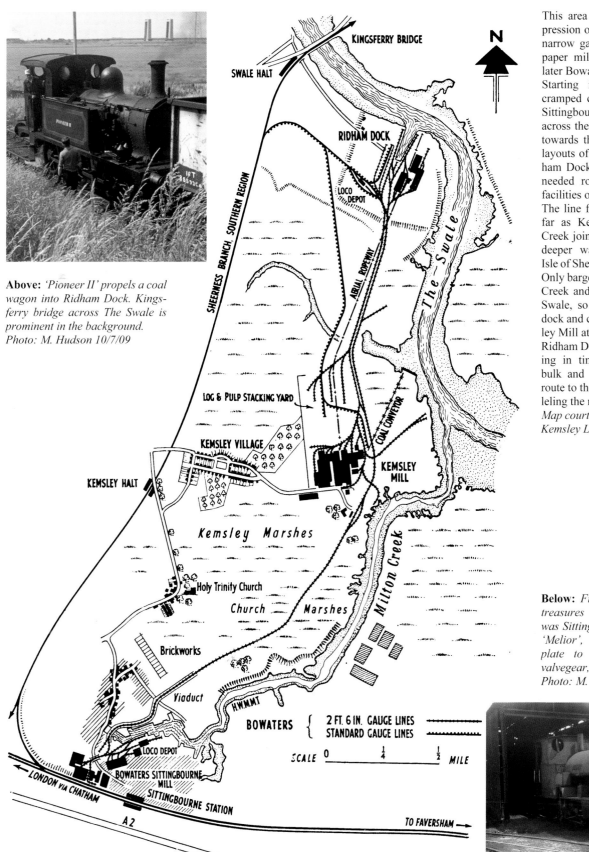

Above: *'Pioneer II' propels a coal wagon into Ridham Dock. Kingsferry bridge across The Swale is prominent in the background. Photo: M. Hudson 10/7/09*

KINGSFERRY BRIDGE

SWALE HALT

RIDHAM DOCK

LOCO DEPOT

SHEERNESS BRANCH, SOUTHERN REGION

AERIAL ROPEWAY

The Swale

LOG & PULP STACKING YARD

KEMSLEY VILLAGE

KEMSLEY HALT

COAL CONVEYOR

KEMSLEY MILL

Kemsley Marshes

Milton Creek

Holy Trinity Church

Church Marshes

Brickworks

Viaduct

HWMMT

LOCO DEPOT

BOWATERS SITTINGBOURNE MILL

SITTINGBOURNE STATION

LONDON VIA CHATHAM

A2

TO FAVERSHAM →

BOWATERS { **2 FT. 6 IN. GAUGE LINES** / **STANDARD GAUGE LINES**

SCALE 0 — ¼ — ½ MILE

This area map gives a clear impression of just how extensive the narrow gauge system serving the paper mills of first Lloyd's and later Bowater's was.

Starting in the South, in the cramped confines of the edge of Sittingbourne town, it strikes out across the marshes of North Kent towards the much more spacious layouts of Kemsley Mill and Ridham Dock. Here there was much needed room to build the huge facilities on virgin land.

The line follows Milton Creek as far as Kemsley Mill where the Creek joins the Swale. This is the deeper waterway separating the Isle of Sheppey from the mainland. Only barges could navigate Milton Creek and the Eastern end of the Swale, so Bowater's built a coal dock and conveyor close to Kemsley Mill at their confluence.

Ridham Dock handled ships bringing in timber and woodpulp in bulk and the overhead conveyor route to the mill can be seen paralleling the railway.

Map courtesy The Sittingbourne & Kemsley Light Railway

Below: *First sight of the hidden treasures of Bowater's railway was Sittingbourne shed. A grubby 'Melior', with her stepped footplate to clear the Hackworth valvegear, raises steam. Photo: M. Hudson 10/7/67*

A Bowater's Album - Sittingbourne

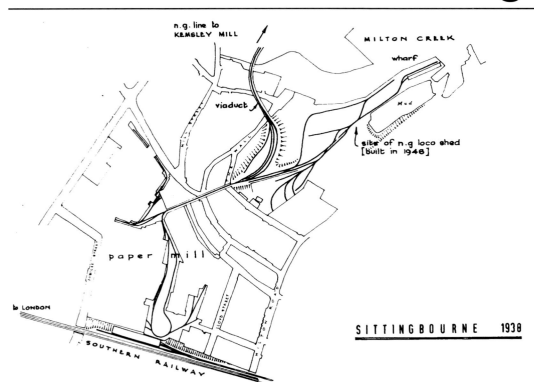

SITTINGBOURNE 1938

A close-up view of the Sitting-bourne end of the railway shows how the cramped site influenced the layout. The mill does not ap-pear to have been built with rail-ways in mind, except perhaps a hand propelled tramway. Curves are tight, with awkward loops and kick-backs to reach various parts of the works.

When expansion became impera-tive it had to be by breaking through the wall and bridging sev-eral local streets (One of which was actually called *The Wall*!). Even then progress was not easy. Milton Creek, which provided an excellent transport link, restricted the site. When again expansion was needed the railway had to be looped round the head of the creek on an expensive viaduct.

Map by R. Ratcliffe, courtesy The Sittingbourne & Kemsley Light Railway.

A Bowater's Album - Kemsley Mill

While Sittingbourne Mill had a Victorian layout, developed over many years, Kemsley Mill was clearly planned as a whole right from the start. Raw materials are separated to different parts of the site with large areas available for storage and handling.

To the North are the log piles, mainly fed by the aerial ropeway from Ridham Dock, but also with both narrow and standard gauge rails to allow flexibility of supply.

To the West are the pulp stacks, storing thousands of tons of paper pulp in mountainous piles. These were entirely serviced by rail.

Coal came into the mill to feed the boilers from the East, either by conveyor from the wharf at Grovehurst, at the junction of Milton Creek with the Swale; or over the standard gauge connection to the Sheerness branch.

On the West side of the mill is the large, purpose built workshop handling repairs to all the machinery and having two bays dedicated to locomotive overhaul.

To the South the steam pipeline snakes away to serve Sittingbourne Mill with power. This helped ensure survival of the railway route after Bowater's had no further use for the railway itself as the pipes were laid alongside the tracks. The future Kemsley Down terminus of the Sittingbourne & Kemsley Light Railway is in the loop formed by the incinerator.

Map by R. Ratcliffe, courtesy The Sittingbourne & Kemsley Light Railway.

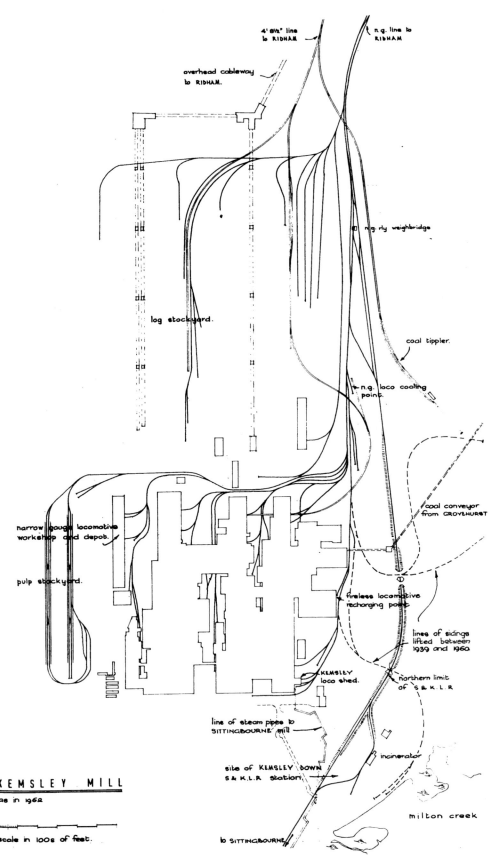

KEMSLEY MILL

as in 1962

scale in 100s of feet.

Labels on map:
4' 8½" line to RIDHAM
n.g. line to RIDHAM
overhead cableway to RIDHAM.
log stockyard.
n.g. rly weighbridge
coal tippler.
n.g. loco cooling point.
narrow gauge locomotive workshop and depot.
pulp stockyard.
coal conveyor from GROVEHURST
fireless locomotive recharging point
lines of sidings lifted between 1939 and 1960
KEMSLEY loco shed.
northern limit of S. & K. L. R
line of steam pipes to SITTINGBOURNE mill
site of KEMSLEY DOWN S & K.L.R station
incinerator
milton creek
to SITTINGBOURNE

Left: *One of the Kerr Stuart 0-4-2Ts, probably 'Premier', hauls a flat wagon loaded with a pair of paper making rollers up the steep slope out of the lower yard at Sittingbourne.*
Photo by Terry Cole, March 1965

A Bowater's Album - Kemsley Mill

This Page: *All is peaceful in the sidings at Kemsley as 'Triumph' and 'Superior' rest from shunting the log yard and pulp stacks. Photos: M. Hudson 10/7/67*

A Bowater's Album - Kemsley Mill

Right: *'Triumph' sizzles in a favourite spot outside the workshop doors at Kemsley Mill while the crew take lunch.*
Photo: T. Cole March 1965

Below: *The afternoon passenger train rumbles through the cutting skirting Kemsley Mill with some loaded pulp wagons trailing behind the two coaches. To the left of the track is part of the large, live steam pipeline to Sittingbourne Mill, while over the top soars the coal conveyor from Grovehurst on the Swale to the boilers at Kemsley. 'Alpha' will make light work of this train, with steam to spare.*
Photo: M Hudson 10/7/67

A Bowater's Album - Ridham Dock

Our last map shows the layout at Ridham Dock. Not shown is the massive flood defence which surrounded the site. It appears on the area map shown earlier, but ran South between the standard gauge loco shed and the standard gauge spur to Kemsley Mill. It then turned East to cross the 2ft 6in line to Kemsley just South of the last siding. Each entrance was protected by a large guillotine type flood gate set into the embankment.

A large area of the dock facility was given over to storing wood-pulp brought in by ship. Arriving baled up into large rectangular blocks, it was then piled up by the numerous cranes into immense stacks which towered over the railway like Aztec temples.

In the canyons formed by the pulp piles even the larger engines seemed like toys.

Down the Eastern side were the two large sheds for storing finished rolls of paper. The tracks seem to run right through the sheds, which is why the battery loco known as 'The Tank' and the small diesel shunter were bought. Steam locos would not have been welcome inside with the finished product.

Between these two sheds ran the aerial ropeway which carried logs from the Eastern quayside to the log stacks at Kemsley Mill. The loading of the each car must have been interesting as each one carried a uniform bundle of equal sized logs and dropped them with a clatter at the far end.

The curved loops beside the Northern storage shed are where the regular passenger train started and terminated at each shift change. The adjacent corrugated iron office probably housed the time clock.

Just off the map to the North East is the Kingsferry bridge which carried road and rail onto the Isle of Sheppey. This was awkwardly placed for Ridham as it spanned the only deep waterway to the dock and a ship strike would close the whole operation.

Map by R. Ratcliffe, courtesy The Sittingbourne & Kemsley Light Railway.

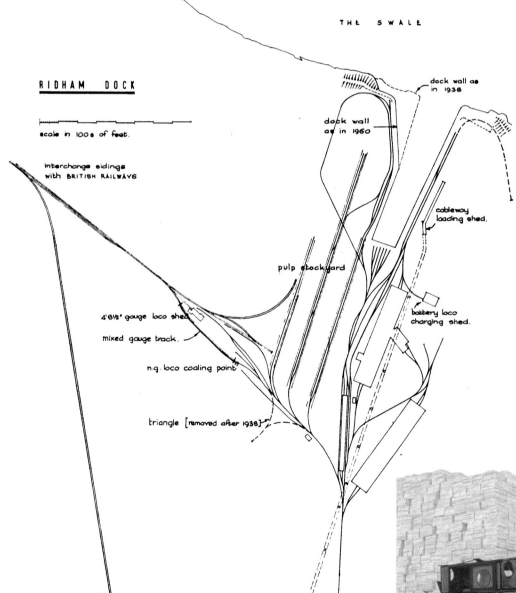

RIDHAM DOCK

scale in 100s of feet.

interchange sidings with BRITISH RAILWAYS

THE SWALE

dock wall as in 1938

dock wall as in 1960

cableway loading shed.

pulp stockyard

battery loco charging shed.

4'8½" gauge loco shed

mixed gauge track.

n.g. loco coaling point

triangle [removed after 1938]

4'8½" gauge

cableway to KEMSLEY MILL

n.g. line

Below: *Manning Wardle 0-6-2T 'Chevallier' stands beneath one of the huge wood pulp stacks at Ridham Dock with the offices in the background.*
Photo: T. Cole, March 1965

14

A Bowater's Album - Ridham Dock

Above: *'Chevallier' has always been one of my favourite Bowater's locos. Despite being second hand from the navy her basic appearance fits in with the other members of the fleet. However, look more closely and she is quite an individual. Walshaerts valvegear and chunky lines make her look modern, but her ornate sandboxes and Salter safety valves hark back to locomotives of the 1850's, and as for the porthole in the cabside...!*
Photo: M. Hudson 10/7/67

Right: *A heavy train load of paper pulp is started out of Ridham Dock sidings by 'Alpha', one of the trio of Bagnall 0-6-2T which were the backbone of the main line.*
Photo: M. Hudson 10/7/67

15

A Bowater's Album - Ridham Dock

Above: *'Alpha' stands at the head of the loop in Ridham Dock with the passenger train to Sitting-bourne. Coupled behind the three coaches are several wagons of wood pulp. Beginning to look rather scruffy it is almost time for her to be handed over to the L.C.G.B. For preservation.*
Photo: M. Hudson 10/7/67

Left: *An aspect of the paper mak-ing industry which seldom gets shown in a railway book is the shipping. 'Ivan Gorthon', a motor vessel built in 1955 for the Swed-ish Gorthon Shipping Line, is moored at the Eastern quay at Ridham Dock. She is probably un-loading Swedish logs as the begin-ning of the aerial ropeway is under the low shed behind her. Astern is one of the tugs which were essential to navigate in and out of the dock.*
Photo: M. Hudson 10/7/67

A Bowater's Album - Sittingbourne

Right: *Fellow Kerr Stuart 'Leader' is photographed on the quayside tracks in the late 1950's. In the background is a large stack of straw bales which would have been carried into Sittingbourne Mill on the chain conveyor which arched over the railway and across the top of the girder bridge. Collection D.J. Hammersley*

Below: *Two wagon loads of bagged cement wait in the lower sidings with 'Premier' in attendance, showing that paper and wood pulp was not all that the railway moved. In evidence is 'Premier's home made, wooden cab rear. This was usually removed in summer for ventilation. The wagons are both from the earlier series with planked floors and ends. 4/10/69*

Previous Page: *A panorama looking down on Milton Creek and the Sittingbourne Wharf from the high level sidings. The tide is out and a barge sits on its flat bottom beside the Quay. The mud is covered with a white layer of china clay, spilt by the crane over many years. Taken six months after the handover of the railway, rails can still be seen on the wharf. With stacks of paper and pulp mouldering in the background and the creek itself the smell should only be imagined. 15/3/70*

Above: *'Superb' makes a superb sight steaming out of the high level sidings towards Kemsley with one of the first trial services of the SKLR. Beside her 'Melior' receives some attention. Both locos have been repainted, but have yet to be lined out. Over the top of everything arches the pipe gantry carrying the steam pipes which followed the route of the railway from the boiler house at Kemsley Mill to the original mill at Sittingbourne. 27/3/70*

Left: *The locomotives water standpipe at the end of the viaduct is decorated with icicles one frosty morning, while the main steam pipe billows clouds in the air from a leaking joint. 15/2/70*

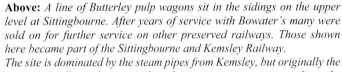

Above: *A line of Butterley pulp wagons sit in the sidings on the upper level at Sittingbourne. After years of service with Bowater's many were sold on for further service on other preserved railways. Those shown here became part of the Sittingbourne and Kemsley Railway.*
The site is dominated by the steam pipes from Kemsley, but originally the truncated pillars also carried a chain conveyor system up from the Milton Creek wharves. This brought bales of straw into Sittingbourne Mill, suggesting that strawboard was one of the products made here. 15/3/70

Middle Left: *'Premier' prepares to take out another trial trip with two coaches and two Butterley wagons. Towering over the rear of the train are the upper works of the two level bridge crossing The Wall into Sittingbourne Mill. The bottom level carried the railway while above it ran the steam pipes and chain conveyor. 15/3/70*

Left: *At the end of the afternoon Bowater's passenger run from Ridham Dock and Kemsley Mill. 'Alpha' waits on the viaduct to be called forwards into the high level loops at Sittingbourne, where 'Melior' waited to remove the coaches and propel the wagons over the bridge into the mill. Above 'Alpha' hangs the rudimentary loading gauge to prevent over height loads striking the steam pipes where they cross the railway. Behind can be seen the viaduct as it snakes its way round the end of Milton Creek. 10/7/67*

Above: *Milton Creek simmers in the summer sun. The crane is poised over a still waiting barge. A loaded trailer stands where pulp wagons used to shunt. China clay was unloaded and stored here, while the ready-mixed concrete depot stands on the site of a small cement works. All this combined to give the creek a slimey white finish to which was added the aroma of wet paper. Just hope this book is not scratch-and-sniff. 28/6/70*

Above: *Steam and smoke catch the early morning sun as 'Premier' prepares for another day. 27/3/70*

Above: *Industrial gloom descends on Sittingbourne Wharf as 'Triumph' shunts pulp wagons and a rubbish truck. On the right are a pair of bogie coal wagons. 3/5/70*

Right: *Looking down from the upper level sidings into the wharf area just after hand over to the L.C.G.B.. One of the 0-4-2Ts is standing outside the loco shed and several coaches are in the yard being repainted. You can see that they must have been constructed quite haphazardly as one has right hand doors, while the other two have left hand doors. With a fourth coach having only a single, central door standardisation was obviously not an issue. 15/3/70*

A Bowater's Album - Sittingbourne

Above: *Having discharged her passengers on the viaduct 'Alpha' rolls into the loops on the high level at Sittingbourne. Here any wagons will be removed by the Sittingbourne shunter and the coaches prepared for the return working. The main line ran to a timetable, with a train scheduled almost every hour for the whole twentyfour hours. It is not clear if all these included passenger coaches, and there were probably others run in between times. The railway was an integral part of the production line and when the mills ran, the railway ran, bringing in raw materials and taking out rolls of finished paper. In the siding sits todays shunter, 'Melior' waiting to deal with the train. 10/7/67*

The Sittingbourne Viaduct has become world famous as one of the earliest used of reinforced concrete. It winds its way from the upper level sidings at Sittingbourne, round the head of Milton Creek, some more curves to avoid property Bowater's (Or Lloyd's as it was then) couldn't buy and then out onto Milton Marshes. Over a quarter of a mile long, the viaduct was surrounded by industrial premises, the gas works and council rubbish dump. In later years it has become a maintenance headache, suffering from 'concrete cancer' which is very costly to treat.

Left: *'Premier' rumbles over the first section of the viaduct with an SKLR train for Kemsley Down. Below is the end of Milton Creek, ahead two of the pipe bridges where the line crosses local roads. The large works in the background is Sittingbourne Cement Works on the opposite bank of the creek. 28/6/70*

A Bowater's Album - Sittingbourne

Above: *Looking across Milton Creek, 'Premier' takes one of the first SKLR test trains over the viaduct. The spindly uprights do not seem enough to support even such a light load as this. The skeleton of a van, dumped over the bank sums up the whole area at the time. 15/3/70*

Right: *A view of the viaduct not often seen. Repair work under way. 28/6/70*

Below: *Clinging to the end of an open pulp wagon while it bounces and bangs over every rail joint is not the best way to take photographs. 'Alpha' heads the morning passenger working near the Kemsley end of the viaduct, where it headed into open countryside. 10/7/67*

A Bowater's Album - Burley's Crossing

Above: *Burley's Crossing was named after another narrow gauge industrial railway, which crossed Bowater's line on the level here. The line was long gone but the name survived.*
'Premier' click-clacks across Milton Marshes with four loaded pulp wagons bound for Sittingbourne. The footplate displays the usual collection of oil bottles and grease tins with their own little guard fence. The sun highlights the holes left in the bufferbeam when the old, curved buffer block was replaced by chopper couplings in the 1950's. 4/9/69

Right: *'Premier' again, but after a repaint by the SKLR. The three coaches has also been spruced up, in red and white livery with a black dividing line. Kemsley Mill fills the horizon with one of the pulp stacks just visible to the right. The log stacks were on the far side of the mill. 28/6/70*

Opposite Page, Bottom: *The driver of 'Leader' is clearly wondering what these loonies are doing in the middle of the marsh with cameras. Another load of pulp heads for Sittingbourne. The main steam pipeline is at ground level at this point. 4/9/69*

Opposite Page, Top Left: *Three pipelines cross a footpath by an elaborate gantry. 28/6/70*

Opposite Page, Top Right: *'Premier' passes under the pipe bridge at Burley's Crossing. Bundles of wood pulp or recycled paper are each done up in their own, neatly wrapped bundle. 4/9/69*

A Bowater's Album - Kemsley Mill

Previous Page: *'Alpha' sets of from Kemsley Mill with the passenger train to Sittingbourne. Behind are at least seven loaded pulp wagons, making quite a substantial load. The spot is beside the Incinerator Loop and was a normal setting down and picking up point for the passenger workings. It is hard to believe that just yards away are scenes of intense industrial activity. 10/6/67*

This Page, Top: *'Unique' was tied to the Kemsley Mill complex by her power supply, a connection to the Mill boilerhouse. This gave her about four hours worth of steaming at each charge. Enough for shunting locally, but not for extended runs to Ridham Dock. Sittingbourne was out of bounds because of low bridges en route near the Incinerator Loop. 4/9/69*

This Page, Bottom: *The sun was very obliging in 1967. 'Unique' seems to glow in it while taking a lunch break on her charging siding. At this time all the Bowater's locos were well cared for and cleaned frequently. Fireless locos had to conserve steam since they could not make their own. To this end most of them had a bell instead of a whistle, which would waste steam. 'Unique's is well polished, and mounted on the front of the cab. 10/6/67*

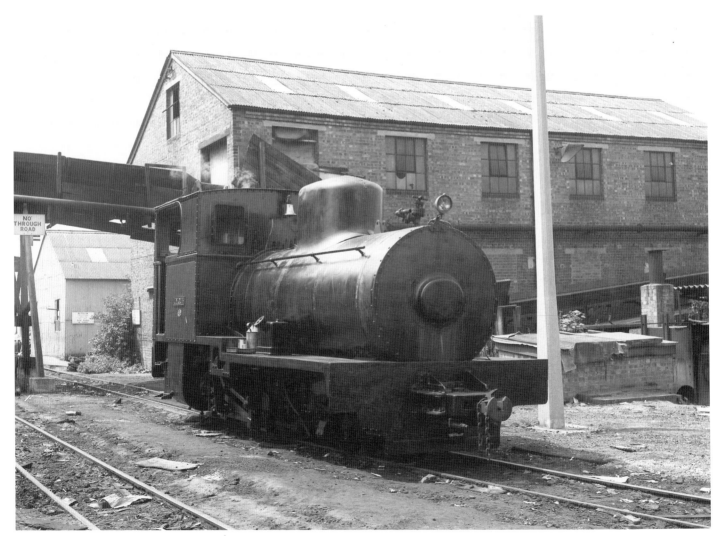

A Bowater's Album - Kemsley Mill

It is lunch time at Kemsley Mill and the crews are in the canteen. 'Triumph' (left) and 'Superior' (right) wait for their return. 10/6/67

Like a praying mantis, a crane looms over 'Triumph' as she shunts among the pulp stacks at Kemsley. When you consider the stacks here, at Ridham Dock and at Sittingbourne Mill there must have been thousands of tons of pulp in stock at any one time. With nearly all this being moved by the narrow gauge railway it is no surprise that it had to be a twentyfour hour operation. 4/9/69

A Bowater's Album - Kemsley Mill

With the cableway in the background 'Superior' is shunting some of the mill sidings at Kemsley. She was the only narrow gauge loco not to be carrying a spark arrestor chimney at the time. The leading vehicle is a Butterley pulp wagon, while the second is a bogie coal wagon. This was used more for collecting rubbish and waste paper, of which the mill generated a large amount. 10/6/67

Her driver gives 'Triumph' an oil round ready for the afternoon shift. From this angle it is easy to see that she is actually a wing tank (pannier tank if you must!). The cab side sheets are carried forwards to give the appearance of the tanks sitting on the footplate. The lines of rivets give the game away. An electric headlamp gives a modern air. How many BR steamers had one? 10/6/67

A Bowater's Album - Kemsley Mill

Right: *An equally important part of the papermaking process were the lorries which delivered the finished product. Much of this was newsprint for the great presses which still lined Fleet Street. This AEC six wheeler, (is it a Mammoth?), has seen far better days and hopefully is only used internally at Kemsley Mill. 28/6/70*

Below: *In the last year of Bowater's operation maintenance on the railway was clearly cut back, or even stopped altogether. This photograph is a good example. 'Triumph' has been shunting in the pulp stacks at Kemsley Mill. She looks scruffy and uncared for after the previous views. A poorly maintained wagon have come off the poorly maintained track, but instead of using rerailing ramps or jacks a fork lift truck has* been called. A quick shove and the wagon is back, but who knows what extra damage has been caused.

Pulp wagon 209 is one of the earliest group with single end brace. You can see where the chopper coupling has been welded into the original curved buffing plate. 4/9/67

Above: *Amongst stacks of bundled waste, poised on the verge of a landslide of rotting paper 'Triumph' manoeuvres a pair of pulp wagons. 4/9/69*

Left: *In a demonstration of what a narrow gauge railway can do in a confined space 'Superior' wheels a train round curves straight out of the Hornby Dublo catalogue. From her angle to the track it does not seem possible that she can get round the bend. Wagon number 615 shows that not all the timber used was carried on the aerial rope-way, unless it was kindling for the loco shed. 10/6/67*

Above: *Close to, you realise just how big the main mill building was. Superior is pulling a train loaded with logs out of one of the sidings. On the right is a waste wagon filling up with rubbish from the mill. One question this picture answers is 'where do you put the shovel on a narrow gauge loco footplate?' The answer is 'on the cab roof!' Superior has a collection of three up there.*

Behind the train an AEC Mammoth emerges from the mill with a full load of paper rolls. On top is the tarpaulin, waiting to be pulled over and roped down. It is part of what must have been a large fleet which thundered up the A2 every day and night to feed the presses of Fleet Street. 10/6/67

Next Page: *They could still build the stacks high in 1969, but they looked nowhere near as secure. 'Triumph' shunts the yard at Kemsley Mill with the distinctive curved roof of the workshops in the background. 4/9/69*

A Bowater's Album - Kemsley Mill

Above: *'Triumph' poses in the sun in front of part of the timber processing plant at Kemsley. 10/6/67*

Left: *Two years later 'Triumph' doesn't look as if she has been cleaned since the last picture. The nattily dressed shunter rides the wagon in traditional, pre-health and safety style. In the background can be seen the aerial ropeway from Ridham Dock. The logs were dropped onto the cone shaped piles with a clatter which could be heard all over the site. 4/9/67*

A Bowater's Album - Kemsley Mill

Left: *'Triumph' drifts across the Kemsley landscape with a flat wagon. 4/9/69*

Below: *Some enthusiastic shunting by 'Triumph' has caused the wagon to split the points. It would appear that an excavator has been called in to put things right. In the background are the conveyors, up which most of the raw materials were fed into the mill.*
4/9/69

A Bowater's Album - Ridham Dock

Above: *One of the regular Ridham shunters was 'Chevallier'. Seen here with a raft of pulp wagons in amongst the pulp stacks, with the electric cranes dipping in the rear. Even though not built for Bowater's her style fitted in perfectly with the indigenous locos. To the left of the train are the separate rails that the cranes ran up and down on. 10/6/67*

Right: *Another Ridham resident was the former main line engine, 'Conqueror'. With her solid, beefy stance, she shared her name with similarly robust battle tanks and submarines. Here she rumbles out of the Ridham Dock reception sidings to return to the pulp stacks in the background. Even though it is hand over day there is still work to be done. 4/10/69*

Left : *The aerial ropeway was still in use on hand over day, and one of the pylons is seen with a bundle of logs passing over it. 4/10/69*

A Bowater's Album - Ridham Dock

Left: *All over the system were attractive corrugated iron buildings such as this office, dwarfed by one of the storage sheds at Ridham Dock. Dating from the early days of the extension from Sittingbourne to the dock, they added a rustic air to an otherwise overwhelmingly industrial landscape. 15/2/70*

Previous page: *'Alpha' makes a vigorous start from the Ridham sidings with a train of twenty three loaded pulp wagons. Each had a tare weight of about five and a half tons. Even if not loaded to their maximum of ten to fourteen tons depending on type, there must be about three hundred and fifty tons on the drawbar. Not bad for a 'little' engine. 10/7/67*

Below: *'Conqueror' carefully propels a wagon load of paper pulp past the long storage shed at Ridham. Members of our party admire her state of cleanliness as she rolls by. At this period all the locos clearly had a lot of attention paid to them. As well as the usual collection of oil cans, 'Conqueror' has a bucket on the cylinder casing, not to mention the firing shovels on the cab roof. 10/7/67*

A Bowater's Album - Ridham Dock

Above: *The passenger train has just pulled to a stand in the loop at Ridham Dock in the shadow of the ramshackle water tower. 'Alpha's crew hustle to uncouple and get on with the next job (or the teabreak of course). Overalls and flat caps are the Bowaters dress code. No posing to the crowd in spotless bib and braces with shiny grease top here. Although the coach bodies were built in house they were solidly put together and continue to serve the preserved railway.*
10/7/67

A Bowater's Album - Ridham Dock

Above: *It is handover day, but there is still work to be done. 'Conqueror' shunts empty pulp wagons through the stacks to make up another train, while loaded wagons wait in the background. 4/10/69*

Below Right: *The water tower and sand drier in the loop at Ridham survived until after track removal. I modeled the scene, but could not reproduce this degree of dilapidation! 15/2/70*

Left: *'Conqueror' makes a vigorous move out of the pulp yards under the aerial ropeway. In the foreground is one of the small huts which guarded the flood control gates in the embankment surrounding the dock. These gates had already been removed, but were massive, steel guillotine type in strong vertical guide posts. 4/10/69*

Above: *This time it is 'Superb' putting on a display as she lifts a long raft of empty pulp wagons out of the loop beside the transfer shed. The lamps at the end of the shed are doing little to lighten the autumn gloom. 4/10/69*

Right: *Many of the Bowaters loco names seemed unusually appropriate. With her massive tanks, bluff front outline and squat chimney 'Conqueror' always looked as if she could take on anything on wheels. At this time she was the most powerful loco on the line. 'Unique' nominally had a higher tractive effort, but only when freshly recharged and had to work within range of the steam connection. 'Conqueror' took her chunky looks from the locos built in large numbers by Bagnall for various Indian narrow gauge railways, with which she probably shared many standard parts. 4/10/69*

As can be seen on the facing page this part of Kent is flat and almost featureless. Bowaters more than compensated for this with the towering mountains of woodpulp bales which dominated Ridham Dock and Kemsley Mill. Dwarfed by thousands of tons of raw material, thrown up in vertical blocks like Egyptian temples, the narrow gauge trains were reduced to toy like proportions.

Left and Above: *'Chevallier' is the pulp stack shunter, moving the bales from the ships to the stack and then from the stack to the paper mill. The older, wooden ended wagons were nominally 10 ton capacity while the newer Butterley steel wagons carried 14 tons. Not much notice seems to be being taken of the difference here though. 10/7/67*

A Bowater's Album - Ridham Dock

Above: *Looking out from the embankment surrounding Ridham Dock there is an uninterrupted view across the marshes to the B.R. Sheerness branch. The skyline is formed by the embankment taking the track up to the Kings Ferry Bridge over the Swale, with the platforms of Swale Halt silhouetted behind the smoke of 'Pioneer II'. Further to the right can be seen the bridge itself, with the two towers which enabled the centre section of track to be raised for ships to and from Ridham Dock. In spite of this lifting section the bridge has been struck by shipping several times and has since been rebuilt yet again.*

'Pioneer II' is propelling its coal truck into Ridham Dock on the standard gauge line from its junction with the B.R. line close to Swale Halt. The standard gauge loco shed was in the Dock, but the main line was really the branch to Kemsley Mill, which brought coal in.

Built in 1910 by the South Eastern and Chatham Railway at Ashford, 'Pioneer II' was a member of the P class light shunting 0-6-0T. Originally S.E.C.R. No.178 she had subsequently served the Southern Railway and then British Railways. In 1953 Bowaters had hired her to cover their own shunter while under repair, then in 1958 purchased her outright. Repainted in a good facsimile of SECR livery she worked the standard gauge sidings until 1970 and was then sold to the Bluebell Railway for preservation. 10/7/67

Right: *In the opposite view the sheds, cranes and stock piles of Ridham Dock fill the horizon. 10/7/67*

A Bowater's Album - From the Archives

Left: *One of the Bagnall trio of 0-6-2Ts heads for Sittingbourne on the famous concrete viaduct. Here looking in far better condition than it did in later years. This is probably near the Kemsley end of the viaduct, where it is still close to ground level.*

Other photos from this collection were taken in the mid to late 1930's, so the locomotive is likely to be 'Triumph' with its longer nameplate as 'Superb' did not arrive until 1940. The original sprung buffer block is still in use, with the coupling shackle visible underneath. Oil lamps are carried rather than the later electric fittings and the lining appears darker than in later liveries.

All photos this page D. J. Hammersley Collection.

Right: *Another train en route for Sittingbourne. Careful scrutiny discovers 'Superior' at the head, identified by her domeless boiler. She is most recently remembered with a plain chimney, but here she is running with one of the diamond stack, spark arresting ones. The site is a long vanished loop and sidings close to the start of the viaduct, called Midway Sidings.*

Bottom Left: *Midway Sidings again, showing how desolate this part of North Kent could be. Said to be the loco changeover point when heavier engines were used. The rails in the loop show no signs of recent traffic in this 1930's view.*

Bottom Right: *Still at midway Sidings, we see a Sittingbourne to Kemsley working. The loco is probably 'Triumph' and the train consists of a china clay wagon, one coach and two flats loaded with finished paper in rolls.*

A Bowater's Album - The Locomotives
'Premier'

No.1 'Premier'
0-4-2ST
Kerr Stuart
No.886 Built 1904
Weight 14.5 tons
Driving Wheels
2ft 6ins
Cylinders 9 x 15in.

Left: *'Premier' stands on one of the raised tracks in the well appointed workshops at Kemsley Mill. The futuristic curved concrete roof contrasts sharply with the collection of old wooden ladders needed for access. After overhaul she returned to service for a further two years. 10/7/67*

Below Left: *'Premier' stands in front of one of the Sittingbourne warehouses in this summer view from the 1950's. Chopper couplings have been fitted but lighting is still by oil lamps.*
Collection
D.J. Hammersley

The first three of the Kerr Stuart 0-4-2STs are most easily described together as they had similar stories. As befits its name 'Premier' was the first locomotive bought by Edward Lloyd for his Sittingbourne operation. It was followed closely by 'Leader' in 1906 and 'Excelsior' in 1908.

As members of Kerr Stuarts 'Brazil' class they would have conformed to a broad set of dimensions covering boiler size, wheel diameter and cylinder proportions. Within this set of parameters the customer could specify a locomotive to their own needs of track gauge, haulage capacity, loading gauge and axle load. In fact the last commercial steam loco built in Britain was a 'Brazil' class 0-4-2ST from Hunslet in the 1960's.

When delivered our trio were to very 'basic model' finish, with typical Kerr Stuart features. The large front bufferbeam carried a curved, rubber sprung, buffing block. Above this they originally carried No.1, 2 or 3, in large serifed lettering. Latterly they were only known by name.

The smokebox door had a central 'doorknob', and securing dogs around the edge. 'Premier' and 'Excelsior' later had them exchanged for the more traditional type with twin locking levers.

The original chimneys were conventional three piece ones with an ornate

A Bowater's Album - The Locomotives

'Leader'

cast cap. Later of course they acquired the distinctive diamond stack, spark arresting chimneys which were the defining feature of Bowaters locos.

The safety valves, mounted on a turret, were originally exposed. They soon gained twin brass funnels to cab roof level. This was probably to prevent steam blowing into the cab, which at this time was largely open. They were later enclosed with side sheets and a new front with circular brass spectacles. The new rear cab sheets came up to waist level. In winter they were completed with home made wooden panels which were also made to cover the side openings. Winter on the Ridham marshes must have been bleak!

In the late 1950's they were all equipped with chopper couplings which were mounted on the outside of the bufferbeams.

Together with 'Melior' the 0-4-2ST would have spent a lot of time at Sittingbourne shunting over the weight restricted bridge into the mill and around the wharves and warehouses. They were also quite capable of handling mainline work when one of the larger 0-6-2T was not available, or the load was lighter.

No.2 'Leader' 0-4-2ST
Kerr Stuart No.926
Built 1906
Weight 14.5 tons
Driving Wheels
2ft 6ins
Cylinders 9 x 15in.

Above: *'Leader' was also under overhaul in 1967 and shares a track beside 'Premier'. 10/7/67*

Right: *A typical diamond stack, spark arresting chimney as carried by all the 0-4-2ST. Shown in SKLR days.15/3/70*

'Excelsior'

**No.3 'Excelsior' 0-4-2ST Kerr Stuart No.1049 Built 1908
Weight 14.5 tons, Driving Wheels 2ft 6ins, Cylinders 9 x 15in.**

To continue the story of the Kerr Stuart 0-4-2T's, Excelsior was delivered in 1908 to the same design as 'Premier' and 'Leader'. She joined them in shunting the sidings around Sittingbourne and later in running the railway to Ridham Dock. Her history follows her sisters until the late 1960's when she was dumped outside the workshops at Kemsley Mill.

When Bowaters closed the railway in 1970 and leased much of it to the LCGB to become the Sittingbourne and Kemsley Light Railway 'Premier' was one of the locos included in the lease. 'Leader' and 'Excelsior' were sold privately. 'Leader' remained on the SKLR while Excelsior went to Wipsnade Zoo.

Above and Right: *'Excelsior' is put out to grass beside the Kemsley Mill workshops. Her battered and buckled bufferbeams, perforated smokebox door, bent handrails and distressed paintwork point to a hard and long working life. 10/7/67*

A Bowater's Album - The Locomotives
'Superior'

'Superior' 0-6-2T
Kerr Stuart No.4037 Built 1920
Weight 17.25 tons
Driving Wheels 2ft 3ins
Cylinders 10 x 15in.

At the end of World War One Ridham Dock was returned to Lloyds from its use as a salvage depot. To work the new, increased traffic Kerr Stuart delivered 'Superior' in 1920.

Although always described as an 0-6-2T it would probably be more accurate to call her a 'wing' or 'pannier tank' as the lower extensions of the side tanks were false. Her domeless boiler is topped by two sand canisters and a safety valve turret, giving her a distinctive silhouette. As built she had an early version of the diamond stack chimney (see earlier photo). This was later exchanged for a plain one. The crew were given a full, enclosed cab for the first time and she later acquired sliding glass or perspex panels for the side as well.

Like all the other locos she was fitted with chopper coupling in the 1950's. To avoid the valve chests between the frames the coupling boxes had to be bolted to the outside face of the bufferbeam. Not the most attractive solution, but another facet of the 'Bowaters look'.

'Superior' was one of the locos sold off the line at the close and went to Whipsnade Zoo where she joined 'Excelsior', Conqueror' and 'Chevallier'.

Left and Above: *'Superior' rests in the yard at Kemsley Mill. In immaculate condition as usual at this time, she displays her collection of oil cans behind the cylinder cover. Being summer time the sliding panels for the cab opening have been removed, but the runners can still be seen. 10/7/67*

'The Tank' & The Diesel

('The Tank') English Electric No.515 Built 1921
Weight 10.5 tons

Above: *The new dock at Ridham must have needed a shunter for the paper storage warehouses as this four wheeled battery loco was purchased in 1921, soon after the opening. Consisting of a large battery box on a massive frame, with a minimal cab perched on the back she was never going to win awards for style. Nicknamed 'The Tank' she served quietly at Ridham Dock until 1969 and was then scrapped. 10/7/67*

('Victor') Hudson-Hunslet No.4182 Built 1952
Weight 8 tons

Right: *The small, four wheeled diesel purchased in 1953 was not much used and rather elusive in Bowaters days. Here she sits outside the transfer shed at Ridham Dock on the last day of operation. The Sitting-bourne and Kemsley found much more use for her and named her 'Victor' after the scrapped fireless of that name. 4/10/69*

'Conqueror'

Just two years after 'Superior' the railway ordered another 0-6-2T. With larger wheels, larger cylinders, a larger boiler and larger tanks it was clearly required to do some really heavy work. For many years it was the main line engine, but could only work as far as Midway Sidings, where smaller locos would take the train onwards over the viaduct. In later years she worked principally at Ridham Dock and from there to Kemsley Mill. 'Conqueror' marked a change of allegiance to W.G. Bagnall of Stafford. Only one more Kerr Stuart was ordered after this.

Her side tanks were full depth and her fully enclosed cab had internal sliding shutters to the side openings. The boiler carried a dome with top feed included and a pair of pop safety valves. Her chimney is a stockier version of the usual diamond stack one.

After closure 'Conqueror' went to Whipsnade Zoo, where she hauled visitors through the rhinoceros enclosure.

Left: *'Conqueror' sits outside the transfer shed at Ridham Dock amidst signs that it also served as the loco shed. 4/10/69*

Below: *A beautiful, sunny, summers day finds 'Conqueror' pausing whilst making up the afternoon passenger train for 'Alpha' to take off to Sittingbourne. 10/7/67*

'Conqueror' 0-6-2T W.G. Bagnall No.2192 Built 1922
Weight 27 tons, Driving Wheels 2ft 9ins, Cylinders 13 x 18in.

A Bowater's Album - The Locomotives

'Melior'

In 1924 the huge new paper mill at Kemsley was opened. To serve this increase in traffic two new locos were ordered. The first was 'Melior', which was also the last to be ordered from Kerr Stuart. It was Lloyds fourth of the Brazil class 0-4-2ST, although she could always be distinguished from her three sisters. This was because she was fitted with outside Hackworth valvegear instead of the more usual Stephenson valvegear between the frames.

All the valve motion was driven by a vertical rod running off the driving axle crankpin. Thus this gear always has a strange, broken leg action when compared to the more commonly seen Walshaerts. The length of this vertical rod also caused the large step in the running plate which identifies 'Melior' from afar. Another feature was the square topped cylinder block, again due to the Hackworth valvegear. In all other respects she was identical to the original three, and shared duties with them. In 1969 she was handed over to the S.K.L.R. and has put in many more years work on her home line.

'Melior' 0-4-2ST Kerr Stuart No.4219 Built 1924
Weight 13.75 tons, Driving Wheels 2ft 6ins, Cylinders 9 x 15in.

Left and Below: *Simmering outside the two road engine shed at Sittingbourne, 'Melior' displays her distinctive Hackworth valvegear and cylinder. Her smokebox door has had extensive patches welded in to keep everything airtight. 10/7/67*

A Bowater's Album - The Locomotives
'Unique'

'Unique' 2-4-0F W.G. Bagnall No.2216 Built 1924
Weight 26 tons, Driving Wheels 2ft 9ins, Cylinders 18.5 x 18in.

Even as the second new loco of the year, 'Unique' was just that in 1924, a narrow gauge fireless with a very unusual wheel arrangement for her type. The steam reservoir (No, it's not a boiler) had to be recharged from the main Kemsley Mill boilers every few hours. This, and her size, tied her to the mill all her life. She passed to the SKLR as a static exhibit.
This Page: *'Unique' is coupled to the steam charging point. 4/9/69*

A Bowater's Album - The Locomotives
'Alpha'

The next three locos to be delivered can be described together as they were identical 0-6-2Ts from Bagnalls, who had become Bowaters favoured supplier. Comparing their vital statistics it is clear that they were a Bagnall design to the same specification as 'Superior'. All the principal dimensions are the same. The first to arrive was 'Alpha' in 1932, followed by 'Triumph' in 1934 and finally 'Superb' in 1940.

Unlike 'Conqueror' of ten years earlier the trio reverted to a smaller, lighter layout which did not have any route restrictions. Like 'Superior' the tanks were really panniers with false sidesheets making them look like full depth ones. The boiler was domed, with a large sand dome either side of it. The smokebox was of the drum type supported on a saddle and topped with the now familiar spark arresting chimney. From time to time one of the trio would be fitted with the plain chimney most commonly carried by 'Superior'.

Valvegear was between the frames, operating the slide valves on top of the cylinders by a rocking lever above the frames. Loco braking was by steam, but the trains were always unbraked, relying entirely on the loco.

'Alpha' 0-6-2T
W.G. Bagnall No.2472 Built 1932
Weight 19.75 tons
Driving Wheels 2ft 3ins
Cylinders 10 x 15in.

Above: *'Alpha' stands in the loop at Ridham Dock with a passenger train for Kemsley and Sittingbourne. Her home made, four pane sliding window hangs at a jaunty angle. 10/7/67*
Right: *The cutting at Kemsley Mill makes a rural backdrop for 'Alpha' on her way to Sittingbourne. This was a recognised halt for the passenger service and is only a few yards from where the Sittingbourne and Kemsley terminus was built. 10/7/67*

A Bowater's Album - The Locomotives
'Triumph'

'Triumph' 0-6-2T W.G. Bagnall No.2511 Built 1934
Weight 19.75 tons, Driving Wheels 2ft 3ins, Cylinders 10 x 15in.

Above: *A broadside view of 'Triumph' in the timber yard at Kemsley Mill emphasises her distinctive boiler profile. Diamond stack chimney, followed by a sandbox, the dome, another sandbox and the safety valves. The silhouette also shows up her short coupled wheelbase which enabled her and her sisters to shunt the very tight radius curves around the mill. Her cab shutter is the deluxe version with six panes and the firing shovel is up on the cab roof as usual. 10/7/67*

Left: *The rivet lines in this and the above shot clearly show that they were pannier tanks not side tanks. 10/7/67*

The three Bagnall 0-6-2Ts became the mainstay of the railway. Their design allowed them to shunt almost any of the miles of sidings and yet be powerful enough to work the mainline trains weighing several hundred tons. In later years one of them was always allocated to the passenger working which gave a workmans service from Sittingbourne to Kemsley and Ridham throughout the day and night.

This night running was another feature of the railway. As the paper mills worked twenty four hours a day the railway had to as well and this helps to explain why such a large fleet of engines was needed. With two or three under maintenance at any one time all would be needed to keep the railway and the mills running. Initially the locomotives had oil lamps, but later these gave way to electric lighting.

A Bowater's Album - The Locomotives

'Superb'

'Superb' 0-6-2T W.G. Bagnall No.2624 Built 1940
Weight 19.75 tons, Driving Wheels 2ft 3ins, Cylinders 10 x 15in.

In 1969 the Bowater's Railway was closed down and many of the locomotives were sold. 'Alpha', 'Triumph' and 'Superb' however stayed on home rails, being part of the collection leased to the Locomotive Club of Great Britain to form the Sittingbourne and Kemsley Light Railway. Both 'Triumph' and 'Superb' have worked again under the new management, but 'Alpha' languishes in the museum line.

As I write this in 2009 the S&KLR sits under the threat of possible closure. Intense negotiations continue, so hopefully by the time you read this 2ft 6in gauge trains will again be running through the Kent countryside with a Bagnall 0-6-2T at the head. To lose this unique collection of locomotives and rolling stock on its original tracks would be a disaster for railway heritage.

Above and Left: *On my visit in 1967 'Superb' was sitting outside the open shutter to the workshop at Kemsley Mill. Since she still looks clean and well cared for she was probably only stopped for light repairs. 10/7/67*

'Chevallier'

'Chevallier' 0-6-2T Manning Wardle No.1817 Built 1915
Driving Wheels 2ft 6ins, Cylinders 12 x 15in.

I have tried, with a few exceptions, to present the locomotives of Bowater's Light Railway in chronological order of delivery. Thus it would seem strange to place an engine built in 1915 after one built in 1940. This made more exceptional because 'Chevallier' conforms so closely to the typical Bowater's appearance. Her size, wheel arrangement, tank layout and even the boiler top sandboxes, all make her fit in with her stablemates.

In 1910 Manning Wardle built two distinctive 2ft 6in gauge 0-6-2Ts, No.s 1764/5, for a nitrate company in Chile. In 1915 they built an almost indentical loco, even down to the porthole in the cabside, for the 2ft 6in gauge Chattenden and Upnor Railway. This served naval establishments on the Northern bank of the River Medway. Sold in 1950, she suited Bowater's perfectly and settled down to work alongside the other 0-6-2Ts. Her main sphere of operations, certainly in later years, seems to have been the sidings at Ridham Dock.

It is only when studying her in detail that you notice her non-Bowater's features. The most obvious is her outside walshaerts valve gear, the strangely shaped chimney and the Salter spring balance safety valves mounted on her ornate dome. The external coal bunker is also different to all except 'Monarch', but her only 'naval' feature, the brass rimmed porthole in the cabside is actually a left over from the Chilean locos.

She has been fitted with chopper couplings, but the mechanism has not had to be bracketed off the front of the bufferbeam, instead it is neatly hidden inside. Chattenden used a central link and pin coupling, but this was probably modified to carry the chopper instead.

On closure of the railway 'Chevallier' went to Whipsnade Zoo with several others and has also visited the Welshpool and Llanfair Railway.

Above: *'Chevallier' displays a very Victorian profile in this view. Her ornate sand boxes atop the boiler wouldn't look out of place on an American 'General' type loco and her flare topped dome with its polished brass Slater spring casings looked out of date when she was built. Ridham Dock 10/7/67*

Below: *Down among the pulp stacks at Ridham Dock, 'Chevallier' pauses momentarily in her shunting duties. 10/7/67*

A Bowater's Album - The Locomotives
'Victor' & 'Monarch'

'Monarch' 0-4-4-0T W.G. Bagnall No.3024 Built 1953
Weight 28.5 tons, Driving Wheels 2ft, Cylinders 9 x 12in(4).

'Victor' 0-4-0F W.G. Bagnall No.2366 Built 1929
Weight 17.25 tons, Driving Wheels 2ft 3ins, Cylinders 9 x 14in.

The two Bagnall products on this page could not be more different. Somewhat out of sequence is 'Victor', which was delivered in 1929. A second fireless loco to join 'Unique' at Kemsley Mill, she was a much smaller engine running on the more ususal four coupled chassis. Her quoted tractive effort was, by far, the lowest for any Bowater's steam loco. This may explain why she did not survive to the end, being scrapped in 1967 after several years out of use.

'Monarch' was delivered in 1953, Queen Elizabeth's coronation year, hence the name. One of five Kitson-Meyer articulated locos built by Bagnall she was the most powerful on the line and ran the main line for many years. The boiler, tanks and cab were carried on a separate frame, which rode on two four coupled bogies with the cylinders to the centre. Steam and the exhaust were passed through flexible pipes to the bogies. A circular firebox without a separate ashpan, was another unusual feature, but one which Bagnall's fitted to many of their narrow gauge locos. After 1964 she did little work, probably being due for a major overhaul, and in 1966 was sold to run on the Welshpool and Llanfair Light Railway where I was fortunate to see her working. After a sojourn at the Festiniog Railway, which threatened to re-gauge and modify her, she is back at Llanfair again. Hopefully this unusual loco will see use again.

Above: 'Monarch' at Sittingbourne 1960's. Collection D.J. Hammersley
Below: 'Victor' at Kemsley Mill. Collection D.J. Hammersley

A Bowater's Album - The Locomotives
'Jubilee'

'Jubilee' 0-4-0ST W.G. Bagnall No.2542 Built 1936
Weight 21.25 tons, Driving Wheels 3ft, Cylinders 12 x 18in.
Above and Below: *'Jubilee' outside the standard gauge shed at Ridham.*

A standard gauge connection had been made with the Sittingbourne to Sheerness branch of the South Eastern and Chatham Railway when Ridham Dock was built. There is a well known picture of Adams Radial tank number 488 in use there during the first world war when it was a salvage depot.

Once the Dock returned to Bowater's ownership shunting was done by S.E.C.R. Locomotives. Kemsley Mill opened in 1924 with an additional standard gauge connection to bring coal in by. The greatly increased traffic prompted the purchase of 'Jubilee' in 1926.

A typical industrial four coupled saddle tank from Bagnall's, she led a quiet life shunting the sidings at Ridham Dock and Kemsley Mill. In 1943 a second-hand Manning Wardle 0-4-0ST 'Pioneer' was purchased as a spare, but only survived until 1954. Over the years various small locos were hired from the main line companies to cover failures. Ex S.E.C.R. P class 0-6-0T No.31178 was a frequent visitor and in 1958 was purchased outright (See overleaf). Named 'Pioneer II' she ran almost to the end, being replaced by exBR 204hp diesel shunters D2259 and then D2228.

'Jubilee' was sold privately and for some time was at the Quainton Road Centre while 'Pioneer II' is now on the Bluebell Railway with two of her classmates, and may well be restored to running order.

A Bowater's Album - The Locomotives
'Pioneer II' & D2259

Below: *D2259 the diesel which supplanted 'Pioneer II' is already laid aside after a heavy shunt. Kemsley Mill 4/9/69*

Above and Below: *'Pioneer II' has pulled 'Jubilee' out of the standard gauge shed at Ridham Dock for our party. 10/7/67*

A Bowater's Album - Sittingbourne

Above: *Sittingbourne shed stands in all its decrepit glory with locomotive detritus all around. The home made, wooden cab back from a Kerr Stuart 0-4-2T leans against the side wall, ash and cinders litter the ground. 'Leader' simmers in the sunlight with a full complement of oil cans in the cage over the cylinders and overflowing coal bunkers.*
Photo: R.C. Riley

Right: *Ambling through the embankment loops at Sittingbourne is 'Excelsior' with the gasworks in the background and the steam pipelines overhead.*
Photo: T. Cole March 1965

A Bowater's Album - Kemsley Mill

Below: *'Premier' and 'Leader' are under repair in the airy spaces of the purpose built workshops at Kemsley Mill. Very few industrial railways can have had such impressive facilities.*

It is interesting to note that the railway had already disposed of 'Monarch', its newest steam loco (see right hand page), but was still repairing the original, sixty year old ones.

Photos: M. Hudson 10/7/67

Above: *'Superior' and 'Triumph' in the yards at Kemsley Mill. Two generations of 0-6-2T built to the same specification by two different builders.*

Photo: M. Hudson 10/7/67

Right: *'Monarch' arrived on the line in 1953 and was the last narrow gauge steam loco purchased by Bowater's. In 1966 she was sold to the Welshpool & Llanfair Light Railway in Wales. Apart from the elusive 'Rattler' she therefore had the shortest working life of any other engine. It is thus very pleasing to include two of Terry Cole's views of her at work in March 1965. In the top picture she is on a feather weight passenger train bound for Sittingbourne in the cutting at Kemsley, while below she simmers in the yard at Ridham.*

She had at least one overhaul and worked almost to the end of her stay on the railway. So why was she disposed of so early? Had traffic dropped off, not needing such a powerful loco? Did maintenance costs finish her? She had an unusual, circular firebox and articulated locos are notoriously difficult to keep steam tight with numerous flexible steam and exhaust joints. We may never know.

A Bowater's Album - Two by Two

Above: *'Excelsior' waits in the Ridham Dock loops with the passenger train while 'Chevallier' pauses nearby.*
Photo: R.C. Riley

Below: *'Jubilee', the Bagnall 0-4-0ST has been hauled out of the standard gauge shed at Ridham Dock by the other resident 'Pioneer II'.*
Photo: R.C. Riley

A Bowater's Album - Ridham in the sun

Right: *A fine view of 'Chevallier' with paintwork cleaned and brass plates polished. The angled plate over the coal bunker has always puzzled me. It seems to be fixed permanently at this angle with wires, but must have made coaling very difficult. On any other railway it would probably have disappeared within the first week!*
Photo: R.C. Riley

Below: *The water tower at Ridham Dock was a distinctive feature of the line. Growing more moth-eaten every year it survived until the end of the railway.*
'Superb', the wartime addition to the trio of Bagnall 0-6-2Ts, displays one of the many variants of the sliding cabside window which nearly every Bowater's loco carried.
Photo: R.C. Riley

Above: *Kerr Stuart 0-6-2T 'Superior' stands at Kemsley Mill with the aerial ropeway towers in the background. Photo: M. Hudson 10/7/67*

Right: *The unique Bagnall 2-4-0 fireless, 'Unique' waits for the afternoon shift to start at Kemsley Mill. Photo: M. Hudson 10/7/67*

Left: *The ex S.E.C.R. P class 0-6-0T 'Pioneer II' shows off her simplified S.E.C.R. livery outside the standard gauge shed at Ridham Dock. On this date she was duty standard gauge shunter and the tanks are being slowly filled with a hosepipe. Photo: T. Cole March 1965*

Above: *Some have suggested that 'Monarch' could not run the full length of the line and over the viaduct because of her weight. But here she is standing in the embankment loops at Sittingbourne having brought a train in from Ridham Dock. As a Kitson-Meyer articulated locomotive she was unique in this country and has found a home on the Welshpool and Llanfair Light Railway.*
Photo: T. Cole March 1965

Overleaf: *Nominally identical, but Kerr Stuart twins 'Leader' and 'Excelsior show many subtle differences in the sun at Ridham Dock.*   *Photos: R.C. Riley*

Above: *Another view of 'Pioneer II' taking water, but this time showing the flood barrier with its lifting gate. The horizon line is formed by the embankment of the Sheerness branch climbing to cross the Swale.*
Photo: T. Cole March 1965

Right: *Until 'Monarch' was built in 1953 the title of most powerful loco went to 'Conqueror', pictured here at Ridham Dock where she did most of her work.*
Photo: M. Hudson 10/7/67

A Bowater's Album - The Rolling Stock

The large volumes of heavy and bulky loads required over 400 items of rolling stock, most of which were bogie vehicles about twenty three feet long. The vast majority were 8 or 10 ton flat pulp wagons with high braced ends. The earlier types had wooden ends with either one or two central steel supports. In 1951 and 1953 the Butterley Company delivered a series of modernised, all steel wagons of a similar size of 14 ton capacity. These wagons formed the basis of various specialised vehicles.

Above: *No.625 a Butterley 14 ton wagon with its distinctive rounded ends, and No.17 an early 8 tonner with wooden ends and floor stand in the sidings at Sittingbourne. 10/7/67*

Above: *No.126 is another 8 ton pulp wagon with its single end brace. In the lower sidings at Sittingbourne. 10/5/70*
Below: *No.8 is a plain flat wagon with special bolsters for handling paper making rollers. Kemsley Mill 4/9/69*

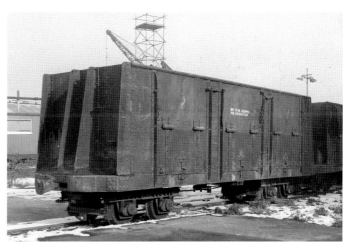

Above: *Stencilled for preservation, but otherwise original is No.2. Built for coal carrying there were at least two of these steel sided adaptations from 10 ton pulp wagons, note the twin uprights to the ends. After changes in coal delivery they were used for collecting rubbish. Both are now with the S&KLR. Sittingbourne 15/2/70*

Above: *We have seen a coal wagon re-used for rubbish collection, but the railway also had a large number of 10 ton wagons purposely adapted for the traffic. The conversions seem to have been done individually, and quite crudely too. A framework with a girder top rail was built onto the wagon and three latticework doors hung from it by loops on each side. The doors could be secured by very basic dog catches at the bottom. They would have run to the incinerator loop at Kemsley, very close to the current Kemsley Down terminus of the S&KLR.*
No.576 and its anonymous partner have both been constructed differently, and a third one on the right is different again. Kemsley Mill 4/9/69
Left: *Yet another variation on the rubbish wagon conversion theme, this time with solid planked sides and only one door. No. 200 (or 300) also shows the American style, vertical handbrake wheel of the wooden wagons. The Butterleys had lever hand brakes. Kemsley Mill 4/9/69*

Livery: Steelwork on all the bogie vehicles was painted black, but the woodwork on the 8 and 10 ton pulp wagons and on the rubbish trucks was either grey or a faded green. Numbers were white on the black frames and black panels on woodwork.

Right: *No.3 is another plain flat wagon, this time carrying a set of points for the fledgling preservation group. The plate welded round the coupler on the headstock shows where this vehicle was converted to chopper couplings in the 1950's. My notes made at the time tell me it was lettered on the other side RIDHAM DOCK ONLY. On the embankment loop at Sittingbourne 15/3/70*

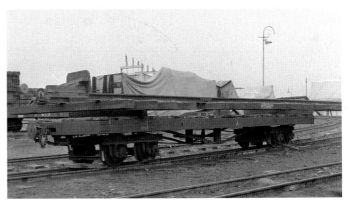

A Bowater's Album - The Rolling Stock

Above: *The railway did posses a small number of four wheeled wagons for specialist purposes. Here is one of several side tipping wagons probably built for coal and later used for ash and similar material. This one has been converted to chopper couplings, but at least example survived with its original chain couplings, which must have made marshalling it in trains very interesting.*
Sittingbourne yard 15/2/70

Below: *Top quality art paper for magazines and books is made by rolling china clay or kaolin into the surface as it is made. The kaolin was brought loose to Sittingbourne wharf or Ridham Dock by ship and barge. Here it would be transfered to the mills by a group of side discharge hopper wagons built by Butterley in 1946 and 1951.*
They were originally painted all over light grey, like No.K30 at the bottom of the page, but K41 has succumbed to rust. I scratchbuilt a 009 model of K41 at about this time, complete with all that cross bracing. I didn't build a second one! Sittingbourne 15/2/70

The dock at Ridham and the new paper mill at Kemsley operated for 24 hours a day and were situated in a remote, rural area. To get their to their workplaces on a shift system Bowater's ran a timetabled passenger service. Originally there were seven coaches built in various styles on pulp wagons. Within a few years of the Butterley wagons arriving five of them were used to build new coaches. All had wooden bench seating along each sides, but there were still three styles of bodywork.

The first, No. 641, has a single door in the middle of one side only. This means it cannot be used for passengers on the S&KLR as the door might not be beside a platform. It has been used as a works and mess car and when the new red and white coach livery arrived briefly sported fake

brick lines like a Southern Railway 'Tavern Car'. It quickly reverted to red and white and is now in the original mid-green with black ends.

The other four coaches had doors on both sides, but on No.657 and 658 they were at the left hand end of the vehicle, while No.659 and 660 had them at the right hand end.

All five came to the S&KLR and have run there ever since. The livery is now red below the waist with white upper parts, divided by a broad black line.

Above: *No.657 is still in Bowater's condition, showing the warning signs placed by the doors. The donor pulp wagon is still clearly visible, with the coach body just built straight onto it. Sittingbourne 15/2/70*

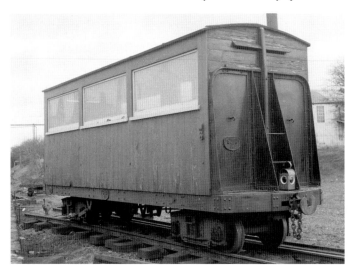

Left: *Something almost unique, a coach side with no doors in it. No. 641 shows why it could not be used in fare-paying passenger traffic.*
The conversion has even left the hooks on the end for tying wagon sheets down over a load, although the road lamp made an unusual improvised tail lamp. Kemsley Down 30/3/70

Right: *A closeup of the signs on the door side of No.641. 30/3/70*

A Bowater's Album - Preservation

I have deliberately focused this book on the period of Bowater's ownership, but the fourth of October 1969 marked the end of a long commercial era and the start of a new one in preservation. Several passenger trains were run the full length of the railway for members of the Locomotive Club of Great Britain who had come to witness the handover of a large section of the track and a selection of locomotives and rolling stock. This became the Sittingbourne and Kemsley Light Railway.

Left: *A highly decorated 'Triumph' pulls away from Ridham Dock with one of the special trains. This consists of the entire fleet of coaches. Left and right hand doors are clearly visible with the doorless side of No.641 next to last.*

Below: *'Melior' ran at least one of the trains. With Kemsley Mill filling the skyline she approaches the flood wall at Ridham Dock. The aerial ropeway is clearly still in use.*

A Bowater's Album - Preservation

Above: *'Melior' waits in the loop at Ridham Dock with the return passenger working. A well known S&KLR driver has already had his hands on the regulator. 4/10/69*

Below: *'Premier' was the first locomotive to return to steam for the S&KLR. Here she propels a coach up the slope from the old loco shed at Sittingbourne to the embankment loops. This was a day of service trials prior to the public re-opening. This area has now been cleared of all signs of the railway. 15/3/70*

Below: *At the foot of the girder bridge into Sittingbourne Mill and under the remains of the chain conveyor from the wharf, 'Melior' reverses in the now miniscule headshunt on the embankment. Freshly painted, but unlined, this job was finished the following weekend in just one day. 15/3/70*

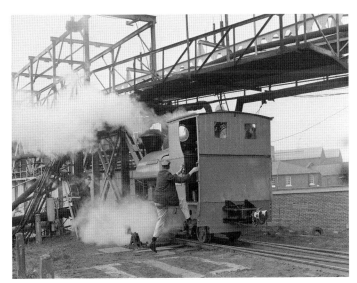

A Bowater's Album - Preservation

Left: *'Superb' brings a test train over the Sittingbourne viaduct. The steam pipes from Kemsley, which dominate the railway will probably disappear with the closure of Sittingbourne Mill. The gasometer will never fill up like that either. 27/3/70*

Right: *Newly painted and lined 'Triumph' blasts up the slope from the shed at Sittingbourne. 3/5/70*

Below: *It is a bright March, Easter Monday as 'Superb' rattles along with a train near Kemsley. The railway had only just re-opened on Saturday so this is one of the first public workings. Behind the last coach appears to be the traffic light type signal which controlled the Incinerator Loop. A stack of rail recovered from the closed part of the railway fills the foreground. 30/3/70*